ideals® EASTER

Unfolding of the lilies,
The singing of the birds
Tell of the joys of Easter
Better than we in words.

—ISABELLE CARTER YOUNG

IDEALS PUBLICATIONS

NASHVILLE, TENNESSEE

My Mississippi Spring
Margaret Walker

My heart warms under snow;
flowers with forsythia,
japonica blooms, flowering quince,
bridal wreath, blood root and violet;
yellow running jasmine vine,
cape jessamine and saucer magnolias:
tulip-shaped, scenting lemon musk
    upon the air.

My Mississippi spring—
my warm, loving heart a-fire
with early greening leaves,
dogwood branches laced against the sky;
wild forest nature paths
heralding Resurrection
over and over again—
Easter morning of our living
every Mississippi spring!

Spring
Alfred Tennyson

Now fades the last long streak of snow,
Now burgeons every maze of quick
About the flowering squares, and thick
By ashen roots the violets blow.

Now rings the woodland loud and long,
The distance takes a lovelier hue,
And drowned in yonder living blue
The lark becomes a sightless song.

Now dance the lights on lawn and lea,
The flocks are whiter down the vale,

And milkier every milky sail,
On winding stream or distant sea;

Where now the seamew pipes, or dives
In yonder greening gleam, and fly
The happy birds, that change their sky
To build and brood, that live their lives.

From land to land; and in my breast
Spring wakens too; and my regret
Becomes an April violet,
And buds and blossoms like the rest.

Photograph by Darryl R. Beers

Little Crocus
Margaret Rorke

Little Crocus, poking through,
Would I were as brave as you.
You're the scout the tulips send
To report the winter's end.
Hyacinth and Daffodil
Fear the earth above is chill.
Underground the bulbets cheer
When they hear you volunteer,
You, who seem to have no fear.

Breaking ground with
   grass-like leaves,
You the snowy earth receives,
Smiling at your fragile form,
Smiling till itself is warm . . .

Warm enough to open up
Your wee funnel-fashioned cup.
"All is well," you notify
Those for whom you are the spy.
Then they, too, push toward the sky.

Little Crocus, I can see
Size of courage isn't wee
Just because a plant is small.
You're the bravest of them all.
They in all the hues God made
Soon will venture on parade,
But I wonder what they'd do
Without you to lead them through.
Would I were as brave as you!

Crocus
Frances Huisman

Who does not love a crocus
That dares defy the chill
And lifts its snowy chalice
While winter lingers still?

Who does not love a crocus,
With cup of brightest gold,

As cheering as the sunshine
To charm away the cold?

Who does not love a crocus,
More splendid than a king?
A royal purple goblet
To toast the infant spring.

Photograph by Pernilla Bergdahl/GAP Photos/Getty Images, Inc.

Through the Veil Torn

Phyllis Tickle

The spring comes so quietly in the country—so without announcement—that I walk into it morning after morning without knowing until abruptly, on some perfectly ordinary day, I think, *It's warm!* and realize that I have already been jacketless and easy in my kingdom for several such mornings. Faith is a bit like that, I suspect, quiet and without announcement till it, too, seeps into our clothing and our decisions and only at the last into our consciousness, till it, too, cuts us loose from chores and clothes and the awkwardness of ice underfoot.

My joy, of course, is in my freedom. The animals are with us again, or I am with them. The fence line no longer holds me separate. I move into their pastures, walking among them as they graze, or they join me in my ramblings down to the pond or off to the close. The world under our feet and about our faces and above our heads is alive again with bees and moths and butterflies and grasshoppers and dragonflies and ladybugs and a myriad of such lives. Their energy charms me, but it is their variety—more infinite than that of the stars—that beguiles me.

It would be so easy, walking these acres, sharing this space, to grow placid and fat of soul—to love these creatures and their haunts beyond their function and place. So beautiful they are to me that only a cross keeps me from the metaphor of pantheism. . . .

A cross, a Book, and an Other who, because of the two, lives so close now that I have lost our borders as well as our beginnings. And each Eastertide our conversation is laid aside more completely, more readily, than in the previous spring, while what has been in history and what is always being in nature blend into that sureness of resurrection that contains both.

Sugar maple branches frame view of Vermont farmland.
Photograph by William H. Johnson

April Puddle
Rowena Bennett

The rain falls down upon the grass
And makes a silver looking glass,
So all the buds may bend and see
What kind of flowers they will be.

April and May
Ralph Waldo Emerson

April cold with dropping rain
Willows and lilacs brings again,
The whistle of returning birds,
And the trumpet-lowing of the herds.
The scarlet maple-keys betray
What potent blood hath modest May,
What fiery force the earth renews,
The wealth of forms, the flush of hues;
What joy in rosy waves outpoured
Flows from the heart of Love, the Lord.

April
Sara Teasdale

The roofs are shining from the rain,
The sparrows twitter as they fly,
And with a windy April grace
The little clouds go by.

Yet the backyards are bare and brown
With only one unchanging tree—
I could not be so sure of Spring
Save that it sings in me.

Photograph by Darrell Gulin/
Photographer's Choice/Getty Images, Inc.

Resurrection
Stella Craft Tremble

The dogwood proudly wears its whitened flowers
As shining streams purl down each singing hill.
The tulip lifts its sacramental cup,
And gold now gleams on every daffodil.
A cardinal flits before us, feather-gay;
Magnolia trees are smiling in the sun:
A cross invites us to a country church
Where we can visit with the Holy One.
I note the marvels of a wonder Hand:
The beauty and the triumph of our land,
And know how hopeless I would be without
The signs of resurrection all about.

———

Now is the high tide of the year,
    And whatever of life hath ebbed away
Comes flooding back with a ripply cheer,
    Into every bare inlet and creek and bay;
    Now the heart is so full
        that a drop overfills it;
We are happy now because God wills it.
            —JAMES RUSSELL LOWELL

*Flowering dogwood tree over the Middle Prong branch of the
Little River in Great Smoky Mountains National Park, Tennessee.
Photograph by Mary Liz Austin/Donnelly-Austin Photography*

April Melody
Mary E. Linton

Another April lifts its fledgling wings,
Another year's new leaves reach toward the sun,
And something bursting in the heart still sings
Through April's tears, of victory to be won.
There is a note the listening soul can hear,
A soundless symphony, a wordless call,
A promise of the glory to appear,
A glimpse the other side of Winter's wall.
There is a whisper, "It will not be long . . .
The time has come . . . awaken and arise!"
And something floods expectantly with song
The waiting heart that Beauty crucifies.
Oh, bittersweet the song that flows unsought
Remembering the joy one April brought.

Roseshell azaleas at Asticou Azalea Garden, Northeast Harbor, Maine. Photograph by William H. Johnson

The Miracle
L. H. Bailey

Yesterday the twig was brown and bare;
Today the glint of green is there;
Tomorrow will be leaflets spare;
I know no thing so wondrous fair,
No miracle so strangely rare.

I wonder what will next be there!

Easter Again
Nancy Byrd Turner

Again the ancient miracle,
As new as though it had not been!
Blossom by blossom, bell by bell,
The south winds usher Easter in.

On every hill beneath the skies,
Where winter storms have worked
    their strife,
April, that shining angel, cries
The resurrection and the life.

I thought I saw white clouds, but no!—
Bending across the fence,
White lilies in a row!

—SHIKŌ

The Splendor of Lilies

Margaret E. Sangster

Oh, rare as the splendor of lilies,
And sweet as the violet's breath,
Comes the jubilant morning of Easter,
The triumph of life over death;
And fresh from the earth's quickening
        bosom
Full baskets of flowers we bring,
And scatter their satin-soft petals
To carpet a path for our King.

In the countless green blades of the
        meadow,
The sheen of the daffodil's gold,
In the tremulous blue of the mountains,
The opaline mist on the wold,
In the tinkle of brooks through the
        pasture,
The river's strong sweep to the sea,
Are signs of the day that is hasting
In gladness to you and to me.

Oh, dawn in thy splendor of lilies,
Thy fluttering violet breath,
Oh, jubilant morning of Easter,
Thou triumph of life over death!
Then fresh from the earth's quickened
        bosom
Full baskets of flowers we bring,
And scatter their satin-soft petals
To carpet a path for our King.

At Easter Time

Laura E. Richards

The little flowers came through
   the ground,
At Easter time, at Easter time;
They raised their heads and looked
   around,
At happy Easter time.
And every pretty bud did say,
"Good people, bless this holy day,
For Christ is risen, the angels say
At happy Easter time!"

The pure white lily raised its cup
At Easter time, at Easter time;
The crocus to the sky looked up
At happy Easter time.
"We'll hear the song of Heaven!"
   they say,
"Its glory shines on us today.
Oh! may it shine on us always
At holy Easter time!"

'Twas long and long and long ago,
That Easter time, that Easter time;
But still the pure white lilies blow
At happy Easter time.
And still each little flower doth say,
"Good Christians, bless this holy day,
For Christ is risen, the angels say
At blessed Easter time!"

Photograph by Nancy Matthews

Apple Pie Bars

2½ cups plus 1 teaspoon all-purpose flour
1 cup plus 2 tablespoons granulated sugar
¼ teaspoon salt
1 cup shortening
2 eggs, separated and lightly beaten
⅓ cup milk

1 cup crisp rice cereal
8 cups peeled, sliced tart apples
    (about 9 medium)
½ teaspoon ground cinnamon
1 cup confectioners' sugar
1 to 2 tablespoons milk

Preheat oven to 350°F. In a large bowl, combine 2½ cups flour, 2 tablespoons sugar, and salt; cut in the shortening until crumbly. Combine egg yolks and milk; gradually add to crumb mixture, tossing with a fork until dough forms a ball. Divide in half. On a lightly floured surface, roll each portion into a 15- x 10-inch rectangle. Line a 15 x 10 x 1-inch baking pan with one rectangle; sprinkle with cereal. Arrange apples over cereal. Combine 1 cup sugar, 1 teaspoon flour, and cinnamon; sprinkle over apples. Top with remaining pastry; cut slits in top. Brush with egg whites. Bake 50–55 minutes or until golden brown. Cool completely on a wire rack. In a small bowl, combine confectioners' sugar and just enough milk to achieve drizzling consistency. Drizzle over bars. Store in an airtight container up to 4 days. Makes 3 to 4 dozen bars.

Egg Salad

6 eggs
¼ cup mayonnaise
1 teaspoon Dijon mustard
½ teaspoon prepared yellow mustard
1½ tablespoons lemon juice
¼ cup chopped green onions
Salt and black pepper

In a large saucepan, cover eggs with cold water. Bring to a boil and remove from heat. Cover pan and let stand 10 to 12 minutes. Carefully remove from hot water and allow to cool (to cool faster, eggs can be placed in an ice bath). In a medium bowl, stir together mayonnaise, mustards, lemon juice, and onions. Peel and chop eggs into big chunks; mix gently with the dressing. Season with salt and pepper to taste. Refrigerate if not serving immediately. Serve between two slices of bread or as a side dish. Makes 4 servings.

Mint-Lime Iced Tea

8 cups (2 quarts) water
8 green tea bags
1 bunch fresh mint
1½ cups superfine or granulated sugar
½ cup freshly squeezed lime juice
    (from 4 medium limes)
6 fresh mint sprigs, for garnish (optional)
1 medium lime, cut into sixths,
    for garnish (optional)

Place water in a medium pot and bring to a simmer over high heat. When water simmers, remove from heat, add tea bags and mint, cover, and let steep for 10 minutes.

Once tea has steeped, discard tea bags, add sugar, and stir until sugar has completely dissolved. Let tea cool to room temperature, then place in the refrigerator to cool completely, about 2 hours.

Once tea is cold, remove mint and stir in lime juice. Add lime juice or sugar to taste. Serve over ice with a sprig of mint and a wedge of lime, if desired. Makes about 6 servings.

Ham Salad Sandwiches

2 cups finely chopped cooked ham
½ cup finely diced celery
1 teaspoon grated onion
⅓ cup mayonnaise
1 scant teaspoon prepared
    yellow mustard
12 slices bread
    Butter for bread, optional

In a medium bowl, combine ham, celery, onion, mayonnaise, and mustard. Lightly butter the bread slices, if desired. Spread 6 slices of bread with even portions of ham salad mixture. Makes 6 ham sandwiches or 24 small luncheon sandwiches (cut each sandwich diagonally into quarters).

Our Treasured Traditions

Remembering Easter

Cindy Hoffman

The textures were straw and dotted Swiss; the smells, hyacinth and cellophane; the colors, yellow and lavender.

The season was spring. The celebration was Easter.

Easter was always warm (or if it wasn't warm, I have chosen not to remember). The new grass of the lawn was shooting green, not in a tidy blanket of uniform length, but in scattered tufts of unruly hair on a balding, brown head. The yard thus afforded scattered, natural egg nests. (At school, weeks before Easter, we planted grass seed in cottage-cheese cartons and set them in the window to be sun-nurtured: Easter baskets awaiting coloring and pipe-cleaner handles.)

Formal, organized egg hunts were unknown to us and probably would not been successful had some well-meaning adult suggested them. Instead, we preferred backyard searches where eggs were hidden in elm branches, on swing seats, under still-dry rustling shrubs, and on the Y-tongue of wagons. Our searches were honest and reliable, the hiders clever but never deceitful. We tried only to be imaginative in hiding eggs for the younger children, not confusing.

Two kinds of children lived in our neighborhood then: those who ate their colored, hard-boiled Easter eggs and those who didn't. Being of the latter group, I suspected those of the former to be vulgar and insensitive. After careful time spent in dyeing the eggs—such clean, solid, magical ellipses—they were cherished until their exteriors cracked and peeled to expose silky, yellowing film beneath, certainly inedible.

The dyeing process incorporated several hours of work. The eggs were delivered to our house by Mr. Bartel, whom we affectionately called "the egg man." Each Friday, he picked up our two empty egg cartons and left two cartons full of fresh eggs, brown or white and—at least, I imagined—warm. As fresh as they were, the eggs were still good for boiling and dyeing. Mother set out the custard cups, and into each one we put a tablet of color. It was—eye-watering and vinegar and all—a labor of love.

Easter is also remembering several books I found so special. The large, slick green cover contained the story of the brown speckled egg and the unexpected friendship of a duck and a bunny, *The Golden Egg Book*. The last line comforted particularly: "And no one was ever alone again." The second book, *The Country Bunny and the Little Gold Shoes*, contained gentle pictures of a lovely, intricately painted sugar egg and the story of a brave, dutiful mother.

In Sunday school (where my mother or father seemed always to be my teacher), I enjoyed

Photograph by Ariel Skelley/Roberstock.com

storytime with the book which had typical 1950s illustrations of a family, perfect and happy and blessed at Eastertime. It was a book of prayers by Peter Marshall.

At church on Easter Sunday, the warm air seemed fused with the heady fragrance of the lilies. On the piano was a bowl of early tulips, red and yellow and lavender. Hands stiff in unfamiliar white gloves and feet in stricture by unfamiliar black patent shoes, I sat in the pew and waited—happily and expectantly—for the miracle.

Easter Time

Marion Schoeberlein

The candy shop bunny
Is all dressed up now;
It's lilacs and April
That kiss the spring bough—
The hat shops have bonnets
That laugh in pastels;

Soon churches will ring
Their loud Easter bells.
It's happiness, gaiety
In every face—
Each heart wears a lily;
The world's trimmed in lace!

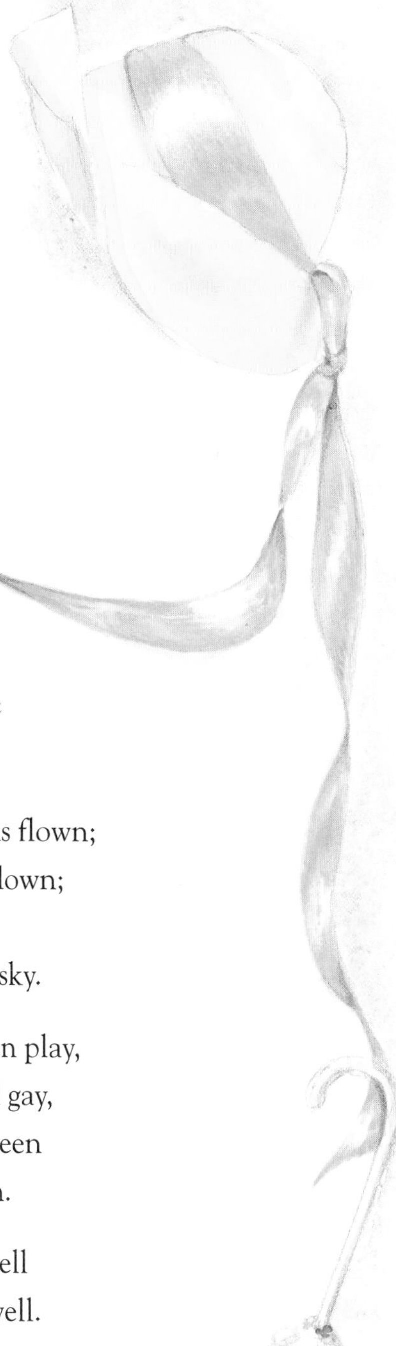

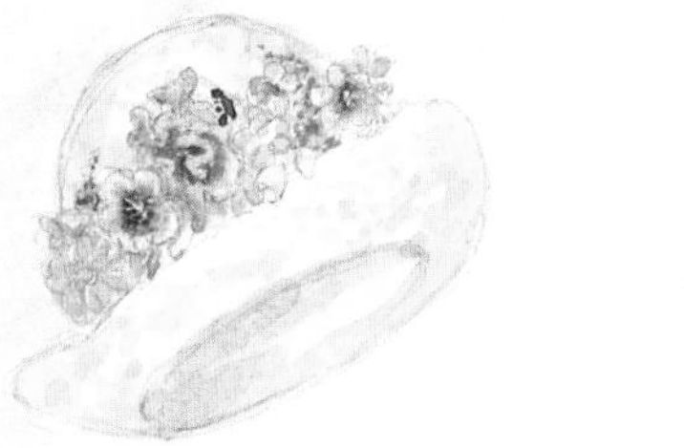

At Easter

Vivian E. Wood

From the garden, night has flown;
Trumpet flowers are full-blown;
On the altar lilies lie;
Anthems soar toward the sky.

On smooth grasses children play,
Clover garlands sweet and gay,
Hiding eggs of gold and green
Rosy hued or silvery sheen.

From the tower, carillon bell
Tells the town that all is well.
All is well.

Photograph by Nancy Matthews

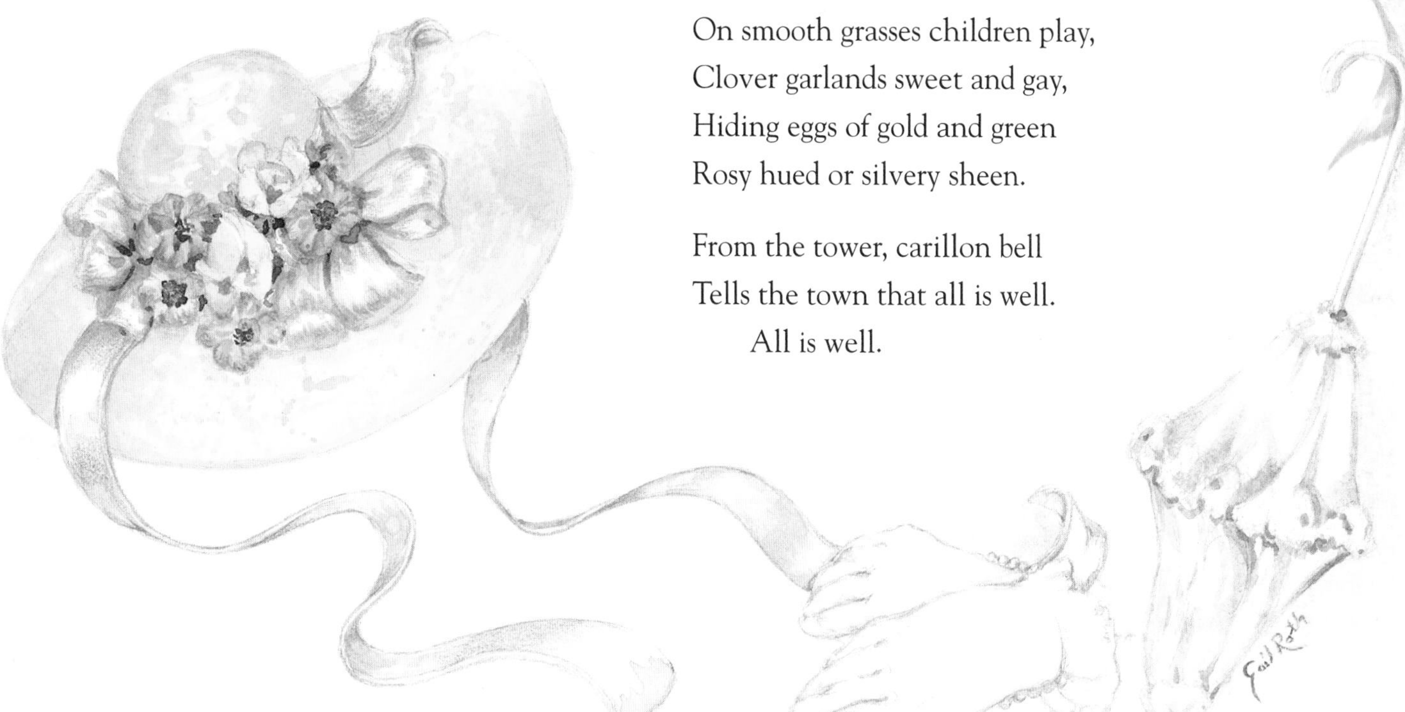

A Remembrance of Easter

Elsie Natalie Brady

Happy Easter . . . what a day it was
When we were young;
First, to church, to sing and pray,
Then later came the fun.

In secret places Mom had hidden
Colored eggs for us to find,
While festive cookies, hot cross buns
Were constantly on our minds.

All week long, Mom had cooked
    and baked
Before the big day came.
Pa chopped wood, the yard was raked,
And everyone pitched in.

When at last we took our place
With friends and family
And Grandpa said the usual grace,
We feasted handsomely.

Then on our separate ways we'd go
And from our baskets eat
Jellybeans, and nibble slow
The chocolate bunny treat.

EASTER TABLE *by Alexander Vladimirovich Makovsky. Image
from Regional Art Museum, Tver/The Bridgeman Art Library*

Easter Service
Barbara Yerbury Filan

April washed the hillside,
Scrubbed clean each woodside lane,
And sprinkled on the meadows
Iris-scented rain.

Robins sang an anthem;
All Nature praised the King
And placed before the altar
The offering of spring.

April
Isobel McFadden

Always the month of April fills
All of our world with colored thrills
Leaves on a tree on a low green hill
And crocus blooms where the sun lies still.
Always with eager hands she spills
Poems of gold on the daffodils,
And behind the miracles we see
Is the caring of God for you and me.

Even the rain in April sings,
Even the blue in a pair of wings,
And oh, the beauty of song that's heard
In the magical singing of a bird.
Even the bell in a snowdrop rings
Of tiny dreams of lovely things.
Even the chords in a weary heart
Sing with the wonder flowers impart!

Photograph by Nancy Matthews

Bits &
Pieces

This spring as it comes bursts up
in bonfires green,
Wild puffing of emerald trees,
and flame filled bushes.
—*David Herbert Lawrence*

The air is like a butterfly
With frail blue wings.
The happy earth looks at the sky
And sings.
—*Joyce Kilmer*

When youthful Spring around us breathes,
Thy spirit warms her fragrant sigh,
And every flower that Summer wreathes
Is born beneath Thy kindling eyes:
Where'er we turn, Thy glories shine,
And all things fair and bright are Thine.
—*Thomas Moore*

Art and blue heaven,
April and God's larks,
Green reeds and
Sky-scattering river.
A stately music—
Enter, God!
—*Robert Louis Stevenson*

Earth with its thousand
voices praises God.

—*Samuel Taylor Coleridge*

Eternity is the divine treasure house, and hope
is the window, by means of which mortals are
permitted to see, as through a glass darkly, the
things which God is preparing.

—*Mountford*

The word which God has written
on the brow of every man is Hope.

—*Victor Hugo*

Featured Poet

New Again
Eileen Spinelli

The robin's song
I've heard before.
The daffodils outside my door
bloomed just as bright
in last year's tumbling April light.

The tender grass,
the slender trees,
budding berries, starry breeze—
I've known these things
across a well-worn trail of springs.

But still Christ comes
to make it new—
new leap of green,
new slant of blue.
For us—new dance,
new chances too.

BENEATH SPRING BLOSSOMS *by Ned Young.*
Image courtesy WildWings.com

Easter Message of the Bells
Isabelle Carter Young

It was a night of lovely early spring,
The kind that tells of beauty yet to be.
The breezes sighed in gentle wakening . . .
And church bells softly tolled along the sea.

The stars of heaven looked down upon the earth
And saw the peace of Easter eve at sea.
The stars sang joyously of Christ's rebirth,
And brought the message of the bells to me.

Benediction
Marian L. Moore

Upon the stillness of the air
I heard the clear tones of a bell
Ring out a song across the land;
I heard an echo rise and swell.

And there against the sunset sky
A cross set forth in dark relief . . .
The symbol of a risen Christ,
All faith and hope and staunch belief.

The bell-notes sweet upon the breeze,
(How near the cross is to a star)
The gentle hand of God's great love . . .
A benediction from afar.

Church bells in the Cyclades Islands, Greece. Photograph by Neil Emmerson/Robert Harding World Imagery/Getty Images, Inc.

The Legend of the Weeping Willow

Hazel M. Deitz

From the dawn of creation until the time of Jesus' suffering in the Garden of Gethsemane, the tree which we know today as the weeping willow was as tall and as straight as the poplar tree. With its slim branches reaching heavenward and its small, pale green leaves, it stood out among all of the other trees in the forest. Many of these willows grew along the banks of the Brook Kedron, which wound its way through the garden. This spring-fed brook, with its cold, pure water, had refreshed weary travelers for centuries. Among them was young David when he had to flee from the wrath of King Saul.

The Garden of Gethsemane was a favorite place of retreat for Jesus. The night on which He was betrayed, Jesus, accompanied by His disciples, sought once more the peace and seclusion of the garden to garner strength for the coming ordeal of the cross. Leaving the disciples near the entrance, Jesus walked along the banks of the brook until He came to the clump of willows. Casting Himself down in their protective shadows, He began to pray. The willow trees were deeply moved as they heard His prayers and beheld His agony. The fact that He was alone in His sorrow made them wish to comfort Him.

Suddenly the peace and quiet of the garden was shattered; and in horror, the willows watched the approach of soldiers armed with swords and spears. In the light of the flaring torches, the willows could see cruel faces as the soldiers approached the solitary figure bowed to the ground. With a mighty effort, the willow trees began to bend toward the prostrate form, thrusting their branches earthward, seeking to shield and to conceal Him from the impending danger. But their branches were too thin and their leaves too small to afford Him the protection they sought so desperately to give, and they wept in angry frustration. As Jesus felt the soft branches around His shoulders, the tiny leaves caressing His face, and perceived what the trees were trying to do, He looked up and said, "Oh beautiful willows, since you were touched by my sorrow and sought not only to comfort me but also to shield and to conceal me from my enemies, from his day until the end of time, you shall be the most graceful of all the trees and your branches shall grow earthward. Inasmuch as you wept with me this night, you shall henceforth be known as the weeping willow, and wherever you grow, mankind will know that you shared my sorrow in the garden."

Weeping willow tree in early spring in Raleigh, North Carolina.
Photograph by Derrick Hamrick/Rolfnp/Alamy

In April
Reuben Butchart

In April—
Was it then our Lord was given
To hang on the rough rood tree?
How could such dolor be?
Did no warbling thrush
The hammers hush,
    That April?

In April,
Can there live a cruel thought?
So remedial a thing
Is the lilting air of spring,
When the first bird song
Holds the heart for long,
    In April.

In April,
How could they nail those hands?
Oh, Calvary's air was sweet!
How fit it were, and meet,
A black cloud's breath
Shrouded His death,
    In April.

In April.
'Tis then the flowers awake,
With the sun, the wind and the rain
Conspiring against death and pain
To put down wrong.
Life thrills to the song
    Of April.

In April.
'Tis then the soft rains fall.
Breath comes sweet in the spring;
Yet, all unwavering,
Love took the blame
On that rood of shame—
    In April.

Photograph by Terry Donnelly
(courtesy of the Washington Bulb Co.)

The Strangest Story of All

C. S. Lewis

We come to the strangest story of all, the story of the Resurrection. It is very necessary to get the story clear. I heard a man say, "The importance of the Resurrection is that it gives evidence of survival, evidence that the human personality survives death." On that view what happened to Christ would be what had happened to all men, the difference being that in Christ's case we were privileged to see it happening.

This is certainly not what the earliest Christian writers thought. Something perfectly new in the history of the Universe had happened. Christ had defeated death. The door which had always been locked had for the very first time been forced open. This is something quite distinct from mere ghost-survival.

I don't mean that they disbelieved in ghost-survival. On the contrary, they believed in it so firmly that, on more than one occasion, Christ had had to assure them that he was *not* a ghost. The point is that while believing in survival they yet regarded the Resurrection as something totally different and new.

The Resurrection narratives are not a picture of survival after death; they record how a totally new mode of being has arisen in the Universe. Something new had appeared in the Universe: as new as the first coming of organic life. This Man, after death, does not get divided into "ghost" and "corpse." A new mode of being has arisen. That is the story. What are we going to make of it?

The question is, I suppose, whether any hypothesis covers the facts so well as the Christian hypothesis. That hypothesis is that God has come down into the created universe, down to manhood—and come up again, pulling it up with Him. The alternative hypothesis is not legend, nor exaggeration, nor the apparitions of a ghost. It is either lunacy or lies. Unless one can take the second alternative (and I can't) one turns to the Christian view.

"What are we going to make of Christ?" There is no question of what we can make of Him, it is entirely a question of what He intends to make of us. You must accept or reject the story.

The things He says are very different from what any other teacher has said. Others say, "This is the truth about the Universe. This is the way you ought to go," but He says, "I am the Truth, and the Way, and the Life." He says, "No person can reach absolute reality, except through Me. Try to retain your own life and you will be inevitably ruined. Give yourself away and you will be saved." He says, "If you are ashamed of Me, if, when you hear this call, you turn the other way, I also will look the other way when I come again as God without disguise. If anything whatever is keeping you from God and from Me, whatever it is, throw it away. If it is your eye, pull it out. If it is your hand, cut it off. If you put yourself first, you will be last. Come to Me everyone who is carrying a heavy load. I will set that right. Your sins, all of them, are wiped out, I can do that. I am Rebirth. I am Life. Eat Me, drink Me, I am your Food. And finally, do not be afraid, I have overcome the whole Universe."

Jack-in-the-pulpit and wild geranium.
Photograph by Tim Fitzharris/Minden Pictures

Revealment
John Richard Moreland

They planned for Christ a cruel death;
Steel pierced His hands and feet and side;
They mocked His last expiring breath,
And thought their hate was satisfied.

They wagged their heads and said, "Lo, He
Would crush our temple and in three days
Restore its beauty. Come and see
This boaster gone death's quiet ways."

They did not know that on that hill
Eternal love was satisfied;
That Christ, who hung there, triumphed still. . . .
And only cruel death had died!

Easter Night
Alice Meynell

All night had shout of men and cry
Of woeful women filled His way;
Until that noon of somber sky
On Friday, clamor and display
Smote Him; no solitude had He,
No silence, since Gethsemane.

Public was Death; but Power, but Might,
But Life again, but Victory,
Were hushed within the dead of night,
The shutter'd dark, the secrecy.
And all alone, alone, alone
He rose again behind the stone.

Moss-draped oak azaleas and church bell at the Episcopal Conference Center in Waverly, Georgia. Photograph by William H. Johnson

The Betrayal

Luke 22:14–23, 39–53

And when the hour was come, he sat down, and the twelve apostles with him. And he said unto them, With desire I have desired to eat this passover with you before I suffer: For I say unto you, I will not any more eat thereof, until it be fulfilled in the kingdom of God.

And he took the cup, and gave thanks, and said, Take this, and divide it among yourselves: For I say unto you, I will not drink of the fruit of the vine, until the kingdom of God shall come. And he took bread, and gave thanks, and brake it, and gave unto them, saying, This is my body which is given for you: this do in remembrance of me. Likewise also the cup after supper, saying, This cup is the new testament in my blood, which is shed for you. But, behold, the hand of him that betrayeth me is with me on the table. And truly the Son of man goeth, as it was determined: but woe unto that man by whom he is betrayed! And they began to enquire among themselves, which of them it was that should do this thing. . . .

And he came out, and went, as he was wont, to the mount of Olives; and his disciples also followed him. And when he was at the place, he said unto them, Pray that ye enter not into temptation.

And he was withdrawn from them about a stone's cast, and kneeled down, and prayed, Saying, Father, if thou be willing, remove this cup from me: nevertheless not my will, but thine, be done. And there appeared an angel unto him from heaven, strengthening him. And being in an agony he prayed more earnestly: and his sweat was as it were great drops of blood falling down to the ground.

And when he rose up from prayer, and was come to his disciples, he found them sleeping for sorrow, And said unto them, Why sleep ye? rise and pray, lest ye enter into temptation.

And while he yet spake, behold a multitude, and he that was called Judas, one of the twelve, went before them, and drew near unto Jesus to kiss him. But Jesus said unto him, Judas, betrayest thou the Son of man with a kiss?

When they which were about him saw what would follow, they said unto him, Lord, shall we smite with the sword? And one of them smote the servant of the high priest, and cut off his right ear. And Jesus answered and said, Suffer ye thus far. And he touched his ear, and healed him.

Then Jesus said unto the chief priests, and captains of the temple, and the elders, which were come to him, Be ye come out, as against a thief, with swords and staves?

When I was daily with you in the temple, ye stretched forth no hands against me: but this is your hour, and the power of darkness.

Crucifixion and Burial

Mark 15:22–47

And they bring him unto the place Golgotha, which is, being interpreted, The place of a skull. And they gave him to drink wine mingled with myrrh: but he received it not. And when they had crucified him, they parted his garments, casting lots upon them, what every man should take. And it was the third hour, and they crucified him.

And the superscription of his accusation was written over, THE KING OF THE JEWS. And with him they crucify two thieves; the one on his right hand, and the other on his left. And the scripture was fulfilled, which saith, And he was numbered with the transgressors. And they that passed by railed on him, wagging their heads, and saying, Ah, thou that destroyest the temple, and buildest it in three days, Save thyself, and come down from the cross.

Likewise also the chief priests mocking said among themselves with the scribes, He saved others; himself he cannot save. Let Christ the King of Israel descend now from the cross, that we may see and believe. And they that were crucified with him reviled him.

And when the sixth hour was come, there was darkness over the whole land until the ninth hour.

And at the ninth hour Jesus cried with a loud voice, saying, Eloi, Eloi, lama sabachthani? which is, being interpreted, My God, my God, why hast thou forsaken me?

And some of them that stood by, when they heard it, said, Behold, he calleth Elias. And one ran and filled a spunge full of vinegar, and put it on a reed, and gave him to drink, saying, Let alone; let us see whether Elias will come to take him down.

And Jesus cried with a loud voice, and gave up the ghost. And the veil of the temple was rent in twain from the top to the bottom.

And when the centurion, which stood over against him, saw that he so cried out, and gave up the ghost, he said, Truly this man was the Son of God.

There were also women looking on afar off: among whom was Mary Magdalene, and Mary the mother of James the less and of Joses, and Salome; (Who also, when he was in Galilee, followed him, and ministered unto him;) and many other women which came up with him unto Jerusalem.

And now when the even was come, because it was the preparation, that is, the day before the sabbath, Joseph of Arimathaea, an honourable counsellor, which also waited for the kingdom of God, came, and went in boldly unto Pilate, and craved the body of Jesus.

And Pilate marvelled if he were already dead: and calling unto him the centurion, he asked him whether he had been any while dead. And when he knew it of the centurion, he gave the body to Joseph.

And he bought fine linen, and took him down, and wrapped him in the linen, and laid him in a sepulchre which was hewn out of a rock, and rolled a stone unto the door of the sepulchre.

And Mary Magdalene and Mary the mother of Joses beheld where he was laid.

CALVARY, *from the St. Zeno of Verona altarpiece by Andrea Mantegna (1431-1506). Image from the Louvre, Paris, France/Lauros/Giraudon/The Bridgeman Art Library*

In the Garden

John 20:1–21

The first day of the week cometh Mary Magdalene early, when it was yet dark, unto the sepulchre, and seeth the stone taken away from the sepulchre. Then she runneth, and cometh to Simon Peter, and to the other disciple, whom Jesus loved, and saith unto them, They have taken away the LORD out of the sepulchre, and we know not where they have laid him.

Peter therefore went forth, and that other disciple, and came to the sepulchre. So they ran both together: and the other disciple did outrun Peter, and came first to the sepulchre. And he stooping down, and looking in, saw the linen clothes lying; yet went he not in. Then cometh Simon Peter following him, and went into the sepulchre, and seeth the linen clothes lie, And the napkin, that was about his head, not lying with the linen clothes, but wrapped together in a place by itself. Then went in also that other disciple, which came first to the sepulchre, and he saw, and believed. For as yet they knew not the scripture, that he must rise again from the dead. Then the disciples went away again unto their own home.

But Mary stood without at the sepulchre weeping: and as she wept, she stooped down, and looked into the sepulchre, And seeth two angels in white sitting, the one at the head, and the other at the feet, where the body of Jesus had lain. And they say unto her, Woman, why weepest thou?

She saith unto them, Because they have taken away my LORD, and I know not where they have laid him. And when she had thus said, she turned herself back, and saw Jesus standing, and knew not that it was Jesus.

Jesus saith unto her, Woman, why weepest thou? whom seekest thou?

She, supposing him to be the gardener, saith unto him, Sir, if thou have borne him hence, tell me where thou hast laid him, and I will take him away.

Jesus saith unto her, Mary. She turned herself, and saith unto him, Rabboni; which is to say, Master.

Jesus saith unto her, Touch me not; for I am not yet ascended to my Father: but go to my brethren, and say unto them, I ascend unto my Father, and your Father; and to my God, and your God.

Mary Magdalene came and told the disciples that she had seen the Lord, and that he had spoken these things unto her.

Then the same day at evening, being the first day of the week, when the doors were shut where the disciples were assembled for fear of the Jews, came Jesus and stood in the midst, and saith unto them, Peace be unto you.

And when he had so said, he shewed unto them his hands and his side. Then were the disciples glad, when they saw the LORD. Then said Jesus to them again, Peace be unto you: as my Father hath sent me, even so send I you.

'Twas at the Matin Hour

Author Unkown

'Twas at the matin hour,
Before the early dawn;
The prison doors flew open,
The bolts of death were drawn.

'Twas at the matin hour,
When pray'rs of saints are strong;
When two short days ago
He bore the spitting, wounds, and wrong.

From realms unseen, an unseen way,
Th' Almighty Savior came,
And following on His silent steps,
An angel armed in flame.

The stone is rolled away,
The keepers fainting fall,
Satan and Pilate's watchmen,
The day has scared them all.

The angel came full early,
But Christ had gone before,
Not for Himself, but for His Saints,
Is burst the prison door.

When all His Saints assemble,
Make haste ere twilight cease,
His Easter blessing to receive,
And so lie down in peace.

*Sunrise over ridgelines in Great Smoky Mountains National Park,
Tennessee. Photograph by William H. Johnson*

Christ Is Arisen

Johann Wolfgang von Goethe

Christ is arisen.
Joy to thee, mortal!
Out of His prison,
Forth from its portal!
Christ is not sleeping,
Seek Him no longer;
Strong was His keeping,
Jesus was stronger.

Christ is arisen.
Seek Him not here;
Lonely His prison,
Empty His bier;
Vain His entombing,
Spices and lawn,
Vain the perfuming,
Jesus is gone.

Christ is arisen.
Joy to thee, mortal!
Empty His prison,
Broken its portal!
Rising, He giveth
His shroud to the sod;
Risen, He liveth,
And liveth to God.

An Easter Vision

Pamela Kennedy

Favorite hymns have been written by evangelists and preachers, great pillars of the church, and revolutionaries, but this is probably the only well-known hymn written by a pharmacist! Born in New Jersey in January of 1868, as a young man C. Austin Miles attended the Philadelphia College of Pharmacy and graduated from the University of Pennsylvania. He obtained a position as a pharmacist and worked in that field for several years. During that time he wrote his first gospel song. When it received a degree of popularity, Miles decided that creating gospel music was more rewarding than compounding medicines and filling prescriptions. In 1898, at the age of thirty, he left his profession for a career in publishing and accepted a position with the Hall-Mack Publishing Company in Philadelphia, where he would serve as editor and manager for the next four decades.

It was during this period that music publisher Dr. Adam Geibel approached Miles with the suggestion that he write a hymn text that would be "sympathetic in tone, breathing tenderness in every line; one that would bring hope to the hopeless, rest for the weary, and downy pillows to dying beds." Shortly after receiving Geibel's suggestion, the unusual circumstances of the writing of "In the Garden" occurred.

Miles recounts the occasion himself in George W. Sanville's book, *Forty Gospel Hymn Stories*:

One day in March, 1912, in the darkroom where I kept my photographic equipment and organ, I drew my Bible toward me; it opened at the favorite chapter, John 20—whether by chance or inspiration let each reader decide. That meeting of Jesus and Mary had lost none of its power to charm. As I read it that day, I seemed to be part of the scene. I became a silent witness to that dramatic moment in Mary's life, when she knelt before her Lord, and cried, 'Rabboni!' My hands were resting on the Bible while I stared at the light blue wall.

Miles continues to describe how, in a vivid vision, the scene of Mary Magdalene coming to the empty tomb at daybreak was enacted before him on the wall of his darkroom. He recalls witnessing Mary's initial despair and then her joy as she recognizes the gardener as her Lord, the risen Christ. He continues:

The first two verses of the hymn detail the scene through Mary's eyes as she comes to the garden "while the dew is still on the roses," and how she rejoices to recognize the voice as belonging to the Son of God. In the third verse, she relates the command of her Savior to go and tell of her experience.

C. Austin Miles wrote additional religious anthems and cantatas in the years prior to his death in 1946, but he was said to have felt his gospel hymns were his greatest legacy. Through the beautiful verses of "In the Garden," millions have been transported to that faraway garden and have participated in the joy and wonder of that first Easter morn.

In the Garden

Words and lyrics by C. Austin Miles

1. I come to the gar-den a-lone, While the
2. He speaks, and the sound of His voice Is so
3. I'd stay in the gar-den with Him Tho' the

dew is still on the ros-es, And the voice I hear, fall-ing
sweet the birds hush their sing-ing, And the mel-o-dy that He
night a-round me be fall-ing, But He bids me go; thro' the

on my ear, The Son of God dis-clos-es.
gave to me, With-in my heart is ring-ing. And He
voice of woe, His voice to me is call-ing.

walks with me, and He talks with me, And He tells me I am His own; And the

joy we share as we tar-ry there, None oth-er has ev-er known.

After Calvary
Marcia K. Leaser

How could he dare intervene?
    To interrupt her pain?
She had just lost her Master, her friend
    and the ache was too new . . . too real.
Maybe if she knew where
    they had taken Him . . . and why,
    she could be more receptive.
But he was only the gardener,
    and didn't understand.
He couldn't begin to know
    that everything was gone . . .
    and would never be the same again.
She turned to leave it all behind—
    then the gentle gardener spoke.
The morning mist gave way to hope.
    Could it be?
    Yes . . . it was He.

Mary Magdalen
Richard Burton

At dawn she sought the Saviour slain,
To kiss the spot where He had lain
And weep warm tears, like springtime rain;

When lo, there stood, unstained of death,
A man that spoke with low sweet breath;
And "Master!" Mary answereth.

From out the far and fragrant years,
How sweeter than the song of seers
That tender offering of tears!

*Azalea gardens at Orton Plantation and
Gardens in Wilmington, North Carolina.
Photograph by William H. Johnson*

THROUGH MY WINDOW

Mary of Magdala

Pamela Kennedy

There were those, she supposed, who would call her possessed still. They would say she was overcome by her adoration of this strange Galilean just as she had been captivated earlier in her life by seven evil spirits.

But Mary knew the difference. In those years before her deliverance she had been driven past insanity—unloved and cast away from "good people." Then Jesus passed through her town, little Magdala, on the western shores of Galilee. She didn't remember much of the encounter except that His cool, firm hand had touched her and the malevolent spirits fled. She could think and speak and dream her own dreams again, and she wanted nothing more than to follow the One who had healed her. If that was possession, so be it.

Mary joined other women who traveled with Jesus, cooking meals and washing clothes, contributing from their personal wealth. Others might have considered it menial work; she considered it a privilege and assumed it would be her vocation for as long as she lived. It had never occurred to her that He would die first. Then one day she stood on lonely Golgotha staring in bewilderment while, on the crest of the hill, Jesus hung on a cross. And Mary could do nothing. She wanted to pray, but could not

remember the words. She wanted to comfort His mother, but could not think how. She saw darkness wrap itself around the city like a shroud. She felt the clammy heat of noon and the tremble of the earth. She heard Him cry, "It is finished!" and watched as they took His body away.

Now, three days later, she stood outside an empty tomb confused and wondering what had happened to the body of her Savior. She had seen a vision of angels, had heard them say "Jesus is alive!" but her mind couldn't wrap itself around such an impossibility.

Hidden behind a gnarled olive tree, she watched as John and Peter arrived and entered the tomb, then emerged, arguing over the meaning of what they had seen. Had someone stolen the body? Had Jesus risen from the dead? They never saw Mary as they ran past her hiding place. Weeping, she approached the burial crypt for one last look inside. Through her tears, she glimpsed two young men. When one asked why she cried, she replied, "They have taken my Lord away, and I do not know where they have put Him." Sensing another presence, she spun around, fearful that the Roman soldiers had returned. She stood face to face with a man dressed in the simple clothes of a laborer.

"Woman," said the stranger, "why are you crying? Who is it that you seek?"

Streamside lilacs in East Arlington, Vermont. Photograph by William H. Johnson

"Oh sir, if you have carried away His body, please tell me where you have put Him and I will get Him."

The gardener's dark eyes softened. "Mary," He said.

In that instant she knew it was Jesus! Joy pierced her heart. She fell at His feet crying, "Teacher!"

Gently, He stroked her hair, then helped her to stand. He explained He could not remain with her but that God would be forever near her as a father is with a beloved child. Then He charged her to go tell the disciples the good news.

Master and servant parted once more, but this time with joy, not sorrow. Mary's feet seemed to have wings as she ran to tell the others she had spoken with the Lord. Some listened to her words and believed them; some still doubted. But this mattered little to Mary of Magdala. For she had seen and touched the resurrected Jesus. That was reality. She knew now that there was hope after despair, laughter after tears, freedom after slavery. There was truly life after death.

If Easter Be Not True

Henry H. Barstow

If Easter be not true,
Then all the lilies low must lie;
The Flanders poppies fade and die;
The spring must lose her fairest bloom
For Christ were still within the tomb—
If Easter be not true.

If Easter be not true,
Then faith must mount on broken wing;
Then hope no more immortal spring;
Then hope must lose her mighty urge;
Life prove a phantom, death a dirge—
If Easter be not true.

If Easter be not true,
'Twere foolishness the cross to bear;
He died in vain Who suffered there;
What matter though we laugh or cry,
Be good or evil, live or die,
If Easter be not true?

If Easter be not true—
But it is true, and Christ is risen!
And mortal spirit from its prison
Of sin and death with Him may rise!
Worthwhile the struggle, sure the prize,
Since Easter, aye, is true!

Large-flowered trillium in Door County, Wisconsin.
Photograph by Darryl R. Beers

Easter Morning
Ruth Johnston Hulse

Clearly the Easter bells ring out,
Calmly the steeple towers
Where reverent people kneel to pray
Among the Easter flowers.

Gently the April sun spills down,
Softly the warm wind blows
And hope, long given up for dead,
A resurrection knows.

Easter Sunrise
Johnielu Barber Bradford

Over hills the climbing sun
Greets the earth with radiant glory.
Tones of copper, coral, and gold
Mutely tell the Easter story.

Jesus stood, once, on a hill;
Once He gave His life and died.
Once the sun refused to shine—
The day our Lord was crucified.

But this morning, skies are brilliant
And the hills vibrate with song.
Bonds of death have all been broken;
Lo, the darkest dark is gone.

A star announced the birth of Christ—
Each Easter dawn a rising sun
Is Heaven's message to wise men,
Announcing Christ, the Risen One!

*Morning fog in Cades Cove, Great Smoky Mountains
National Park, Tennessee. Photograph by Terry
Donnelly/Donnelly-Austin Photography*

The Easter Message

Charles E. Hesselgrave

No more significant, spontaneous, or universally attractive festival has ever been instituted than that which celebrates the return of spring, the budding of leaves and flowers, and the triumphant hope that eternally beckons forward the human race. Older than Christianity and deeply rooted in the love of life itself, the spirit of Easter finds its most perfect expression in the Resurrection story of Jesus. There is, indeed, good cheer in the sight of flowers lifting their faces once more toward the sunlight, after the frosts and storms of winter have spent their force. The swelling seeds and changing tints of green give promise of the coming harvests and assure us of nature's ready response to our physical needs. The songs of the birds and the humming of the bees remind us of the rising tide of life that surrounds us and through countless channels is rushing onward with the pulse beat of recurring years. In all this stir of creative energy, this bursting of winter's fetters and the renewal of life's struggle for undisputed supremacy, we feel a kindling interest and secret joy, which carry us outside the old limitations and broaden the horizons of our purposes and hopes.

But did the springtime come and go with no other message of inspiration, the world of mankind would grow old and weary and discouraged with its toil and disappointment, its wasting wars and ceaseless oppressions, its heroic attempts and saddening failures, and the oft recurring sight of its shining ideals cast to the earth and trampled upon by the gross feet of selfishness and indifference. Humanity knows but too well its own weakness and defects.

Memory, as well as science, reminds us that one spring is like another, that man's life, too, is but a coming and a going, as the budding spring burts into summer and comes at last to rest beneath winter's snow. But Easter adds the everlasting crown to man's hope and inspiration in the Resurrection story. Therein we pass from intimations of nature into the realm of human struggle and aspiration where the organizing forces of life surge to and fro with tragic consequence and man more often questions the worth of the final result.

Back to the Gospel source go those whose faith in human possibilities and courage for unmeasured tasks must needs be renewed in some lifegiving stream. Not only in the buds and blossoms may we see the victory of life, but also in the story of Calvary and the Garden, where we find goodness and righteousness eternally triumphant over villainy and injustice, non-resistence over aggression, humility over pride, holiness over sin, love over hate. We are assured that though evil may hold the reins for a season, dominion and power belong ultimately to justice and right. However complete may be the temporary defeat of truth, error shall not always abide.

Easter proclaims that man shall overcome all his foes, including death itself. His pathway may lead him through the sorrows of Gethsemane, the pain and darkness of Calvary; nevertheless his winter of distress will yet turn to the spring of delight, defeat will be forgotten in the joy of final victory, and the life of the spirit will rise in glory from the shadows of the grave.

The First Church of Lincoln and flowering dogwoods in Lincoln, Massachusetts. Photograph by William H. Johnson

Rejoice and Be Glad
Emily May Young

For springtime's warmth this Easter morn,
For bright-hued flowers, fresh, newborn,
My heart is now rejoicing.

For cobalt skies and emerald hills,
For myriad songbirds' happy trills,
My heart is now rejoicing.

For Easter lilies blooming where
All reverent heads are bent in prayer,
My heart is now rejoicing.

For Christ, who came to point the way,
Who died, arose, and lives today,
My heart is now rejoicing.

Ye Heav'ns, Uplift Your Voice
Author Unkown

Ye heav'ns uplift your voice;
Sun, moon, and stars, rejoice;
And thou, too, nether earth,
Join in the common mirth:
For winter storm at last,
And rain is over-past:
Instead whereof the green
And fruitful palm is seen.

Ye birds with open throat
Prolong your sweetest note;
Awake, ye blissful quires,
And strike your merry lyres:
For why? unhurt by Death,
The Lord of life and breath,
Jesus, as He foresaid,
Is risen from the dead.

Ye flow'rs of Spring, appear;
Your gentle heads uprear,
And let the growing seed
Enamel lawn and mead.
Ye roses inter-set
With clumps of violet,
Ye lilies white, unfold
In beds of marigold.

*Iris at the edge of Red House Lake, Allegany State
Park, New York. Photograph by Carr Clifton*

O Glorious Easter morning!
O day of peace and light!
One precious name adorning
With lilies pure and white,
A gladsome message bringing
Of love that knows no fear;
The sweetest anthem singing:
"The risen Christ is here."

—SARAH K. BOLTON

IISBN-13: 978-0-8249-1324-3

Published by Ideals Publications, a Guideposts Company
Nashville, Tennessee
www.idealsbooks.com

Publisher, Peggy Schaefer
Editor, Melinda L. R. Rumbaugh
Copy Editor, Kaye Dacus
Designer, Marisa Jackson
Permissions Editor, Patsy Jay

Cover: *Victorian Seasons—Spring* by Susan Bourdet. Painting courtesy www.wildwings.com
Inside front cover: Painting by George Hinke. Image from Ideals Publications
Inside back cover: Painting by George Hinke. Image from Ideals Publications
Additional art credits: "Bits & Pieces" and "Family Recipes" art by Kathy Rusynyk

"In the Garden" sheet music by Dick Torrans, Melode, Inc.

ACKNOWLEDGMENTS:

BENNETT, ROWENA BASTIN. "April Puddle" from *Boys and Girls Today*, May 1941, The Methodist Publishing House. Courtesy of Kenneth C. Bennett. LEWIS, C. S. "The Strangest Story of All" from *God In the Dock* by C. S. Lewis, copyright © C.S. Lewis Pte. Ltd. 1970. Extract reprinted by permission. LINTON, MARY E. "April Melody" from *Roads Wide With Wonder* by Mary E. Linton. Used by permission of Richard W. Kobelt. MCFADDEN, ISOBEL. "April" from *Reward and Other Poems* by Isobel McFadden. Published by Ryerson Press, Canada. MEYNELL, ALICE. "Easter Night" from *Our Holidays in Poetry*, published by H. W. Wilson Co., 1929. RORKE, MARGARET L. "Little Crocus" from *An Old Cracked Cup*. Copyright © 1980 by author. Used by permission of Margaret Ann Rorke. TICKLE, PHYLLIS. "Through the Veil Torn" from *Wisdom in the Waiting: Spring's Sacred Days* by Phyllis Tickle (Loyola Press, 2004). Reprinted by permission of Loyola Press. TREMBLE, STELLA CRAFT. "Resurrection" from *Happy Holidays, Vol. II* by Stella Craft Tremble. Used by permission of Eleanor V. Tremble. TURNER, NANCY BYRD. "Easter Again" from *Silver Saturday*. Copyright © 1937 by Nancy Byrd Turner. Used by permission of Margaret Fleury Hutcheson. WALKER, MARGARET. "My Mississippi Spring" from *This Is My Century: New and Collected Poems* by Margaret Walker. Copyright © 1989 by Margaret Walker Alexander. Used by permission of the University of Georgia Press. OUR THANKS to the following authors or their heirs: Henry H. Barstow, Johnielu Barber Bradford, Elsie N. Brady, Hazel M. Deitz, Barbara Yerbury Filan, Cindy Hoffman, Frances Huisman, Ruth Johnston Hulse, Pamela Kennedy, Marcia Krugh Leaser, Marian L. Moore, John Richard Moreland, Marion Schoeberlein, Eileen Spinelli, Vivian E. Wood, Isabelle Carter Young and Emily May Young.

Every effort has been made to establish ownership and use of each selection in this book. If contacted, the publisher will be pleased to rectify any inadvertent errors or omissions in subsequent editions.